Katrine Lynn Solvaag is a Norwegian performance poet based in Canterbury, where she is currently completing her MA in Creative Writing. She has performed at an array of festivals, including Brighton Fringe and Wise Words, and is currently the founder and editor-in-chief of *Dissonance Magazine*. During her bachelor's degree, Katrine undertook a high volume of volunteer work as society president and festival organiser. In 2017 the university rewarded her dedication with the Kent Student Award for Outstanding Contribution to Arts and Culture.

Broken People

Katrine Lynn Solvaag

Burning Eye

Broken People

CONTENTS

THE HEALING

THE BREAKING

THE MORNING AFTER

Hello.
Have a seat.
How are you?

I'm just going to ask you a few questions.

How old are you?
What's the first initial of your first name?
What's the first initial of your last name?
Can you tell me the beginning of your postcode?

When did the incident occur?
What time exactly?

When did you last have your period?
And that was the day it started?
How long did that period last?
Is that length normal for you?
Have you taken it anytime since your last period?

Are you currently taking any medication?
Do you have any allergies?
Do you have any serious health conditions?
Have you had any serious illnesses or injuries in the past?

Do you use any form of contraception?
Have you considered any other?
Have you considered the pill?

You have to take this as soon as possible.
If you throw up within two hours of taking this,
you will have to come back right away and take another,
as your body wouldn't have had time to absorb it.

If your period is more than five days late,
you should consider taking a pregnancy test.

If you haven't had your period within ten days
of expecting it or if it is lighter or shorter than normal,
you should contact your local GP for an appointment
immediately.

If you are already pregnant,
this should not harm your baby.

There you go.
Hope you have a good day.

SHOEBOX SECRETS

How could I have known? Did you know? I think I lost the brochure explaining my rights. Or did I ever get it?

'I now know what honest people talking about a situation that victimised them sound like,' she says, her eyes travelling back and forth through the court room like it's a game of tennis. She's only ten.

'That isn't the correct form of feminism,' a tabloid whispers. 'She's entitled, she's got money, she's white, she's famous, she's...' They fail to point out that she is a woman. That she is a victim who only spoke up two years later when the man who assumed his right to her body came back to place the blame of his failed life on her.

Why are women always to blame?

I feel sick reading the comment sections.

I never knew. Did you? Haven't we all felt that unexpected touch as an unseen hand tucked itself within our skirts and pinched the bum beneath? There is no need to keep your secrets from me. Did you know that can be considered sexual assault? Why do we live with this?

For me it was in a nightclub. I was smiling, dancing, laughing with friends, singing *we are young and free*. Apparently he confused freedom with the liberty to touch my body. I never saw who it was. I didn't tell my friends, didn't want to ruin the mood, to cause a scene. So I danced, but my smile had been robbed from me.

Do you hear that? The laughter, the cat-calls, the whistles as you walk along the street. Why do they assume the right to comment on my body? Have I asked for their opinion?

Can you still see their eyes? Burnt within your retina as they undress you with their minds. I'm wearing a big, puffy coat, my legs bare in the warming winter sun. The postman stares. Why is he staring? It was only supposed to be a short walk around the block. They say fresh air is good for you. Why is he still staring? Should I say something? No, just walk, ignore him, forget it ever happened. But you never forgot, did you?

We are fifty-one percent of the population. There are more of us than of them. So why do we feel so scared?

Why should a ten-year-old girl need to know the voice of a victim? Is she so doomed to relive the horrors of those who came before? Is there even a single woman out there who has not been forced to play the role of victim at one point in her life? If so, speak up. What is your secret?

I bury mine in a shoebox beneath my bed. Transcribed in ink within a pink diary – all those nasty moments left unsaid: the shadows, the stares, the glares, the touch. He followed me for fifteen minutes along the dark streets. I was petrified. Could he smell my fear? Could he see me frantically trying to call a familiar face and reaching voicemail? Did he count the number of times I turned around to check if he was still there, fifteen feet behind? Did that turn him on?

I've spent my life hiding from shadows. 'Let me walk you home,' a male friend would insist. Why do I have to fear the night more than him?

A MODERN-ERA PHANTOM

I am a ghost
but not the kind you can discover with a plasma detector
nor find in the creak of wood worn by time
I am an unnoticed breeze rushing through trees
the rattling of amber leaves
making friends with squirrels

I am an idea which never drew its first breath
the contrast between birdsong and firecrackers
shoved down skeletal throats

I am the voices the world never bothered to hear
overpowered by the loading of guns
and the *pah-pah-pah* of war. even our gods
have ceased to listen to our cries of *no more*
with our chests pressed against gravel

I am every single nightmare and sweet dream equally:
the love you never confessed, the thoughts
at the back of your mind. I am the one
who teaches children how to scream
in hope to spare them from dark-tinted vans
I don't always succeed

I was raped by the devil in disguise as a teenage boy
not confused but abusive as he crawled into my bed
and made himself at home in my body
I am every unreported crime in fear
of having to explain my violation
to a stranger

I am the anxieties of a boy too afraid
to tell his parents he does not like girls
fearing the disappointment in his mother's eyes
and his father's reactionary speech on how
men in ancient times did not make love to other men

I am the ghost of unspoken words fluttering
within a million hearts, a stomach
filled with decomposing butterflies
the distance between lovers kept apart

I am the one we do not speak of
the horrors of lands whose names we dare not pronounce
whose existence we denounce
simply because we don't have time
because we can no longer comprehend numbers
as people

I am blood spilt and dried to a crust
children taught not to trust. I am every broken heart
and broken bone gone unnoticed

I am a ghost
but you've never heard of me
I'm the nagging thought at the back of your mind
you will never catch

I will always remain invisible

DEPRESSION'S PLAYGROUND

please can you listen to me instead of that douchebag?
          is what my Sanity tries to say
as Depression comes out to play with his array
of self-destruct advice and plans to hijack
the control panel in my brain because
he's in the mood to have some fun again

he uses the microphone
to dictate my thoughts and knead my heart
into knots compressing my emotions
until they become explosive

corrosive
as I erode away
he proposes fantasies of escaping to sea
with rocks

technology is amazing!
for with the click of a button
I no longer yearn for sunshine days
but rather dim-lit hallways, caught
in a self-made maze of confusion

my gaze hindered by Hope running away
in the opposite direction
bringing with her the ability to feel affection
as I am left numb
this heart plumb unable to strum
without the added lubrication of rum

you asked me what I meant when I said I was numb
it means I am unable to feel the words *I love you*

it means I am willing to let go of life and watch
as it drifts away like balloons into a distant sky
Mom always said they'd find a better life
but all I find is my hand wrapped around a knife

designed to sever every healthy tie still remaining in my life

it's not you, it's me
will always remain a mockery
please don't allow me to break
down and crumble
scramble this jumble of an existence
into nothing

please know I'm bluffing
when I say I no longer love you
huffing and puffing hollow words to hurt
because I want you to know there is pain
inside this vacant cavity

as I fight a losing battle against gravity
staying longer and longer
in bed each morning

TIDAL WAVE

I remember the silence
the moment before when the world forgot its friction
and for a fractured second stood still

I watched as the ocean retreated away from the shore
unsure of where it was heading

regretting my static statue I upheaved my feet
and followed

what happened next is a blur
my mind caught in a continual stir of whispered droplets
colliding with my sockets
blinding me

I feel like I'm drowning but there is no water in my lungs

my tongue has lost the ability to scream or even heave
as I find myself breathing out drained hope
and in an empty promise

I have become diadromous
shifting between seas like seasons
you can see me slithering through the crowd
before I slip away

slowly losing my grip on life
on my disguise of *I'm okay*
misplacing my will to emerge
from the tidal wave that is my duvet

I am trapped
between blankets and pillows
these soft entities the symptoms
my mind wants to erase away
as it heads down a highway
towards oblivion

the dictionary is drained of words
to convey this hollowness
this *how-to*-ness, this mess
this nest of hopelessness
as I huddle down and rock
in rhythm to the drifting waves

I'm told to wait this phase out
to not let doubt in existence create distance
between me and my surroundings
while my pounding rabbit-heart tries
to figure its way out of this maze

but when trapped in water
everything looks the same

days   weeks months
maybe even years pass by
within this time I've learned to speak to fish
their pouting lips giving kisses whenever I feel low
and their glowing bodies granting light in this dark dwelling

one day their colours compel me to follow
as we wallow together towards a new current
which rips and pulls us astray to a stranger place
and before I know it I can see shore again

it's a slow process
each step towards recovery
a rediscovery of myself
a battle against the waves trying to pull me away
but I'm here

I can hear the seagulls cry
and I smile knowing I've survived
another tidal wave

DINNERTIME PROTEST

I will not lower my voice.

I will not file down my edges simply because my sharpness happens to poke you in the side. I will not apologise for traits childhood rooted in my mind. I will not *soften* myself just because it suits your bullying, to allow you ease when you stretch out and breathe in my oxygen directly from my lungs.

Do not confuse me with playdough – I am not a mould awaiting your dirty hands to grasp and shape my body to the image of your desires. I do not exist to make your existence more pleasant. I am not a trophy for your eyes, neither a blur in the dark you can force on its knees and plead to take your phallic power in its mouth.

Be aware: this bitch is not afraid to bite.

Don't you dare paint me as rude for not being weak, for not bending over when you speak, for not begging you to pardon me when my dreams happened to inconvenience you.

My arms are open to every kind heart – to every soul who knows what it's like to be belittled, to be brushed off like an insignificant crumb, to be regarded as something which needs to be fixed, to be swatted and crushed like a bluebottle fly.

I want the people I meet to be unapologetic. I want them to shine and glitter with everything that makes them unique. I never want to see someone dissolve beneath another's touch. Our shared air is too valuable to be crumpled by ego.

So the next time you ask me to lower my voice, to be more ladylike, to avoid that snark in my tone after you so hypocritically behaved the same way as me, I will stamp my feet and slam on my chest like a gorilla until you creak away.

You do not have a say in how I live my life nor what I do with my body, and I will *never* lower my voice until it becomes unnecessary for me to *scream* just in order to be *heard*.

CHRYSLER

there

is something

rotten within this

nectarine its pit moulded

transmuted into
maggots focused on
nurturing egos emerging
from dirt their charcoal
exterior concealing chemical
spills leaking into rivers

bluebell dust the new
E. coli as it spreads
inside skyscrapers long left
empty due to polar bear
politicians deciding humans
weren't worth saving while
water rose above aesthetic
expression

Chrysler you are betrayed
enclosed within your water
frame your art deco
edifice corroding among a
polluted sea and poisoned
fish

WHY HURRICANES ARE NAMED AFTER PEOPLE

you   leave me restless
not like an itching dog with fleas
but a breathless hummingbird
fleeing fleeting emotions
strong like crashing waves
not wanting to wait on the stroke
that will crush me

you're the hurricane and I'm the house
awaiting each nail and plank to be stripped off
my silhouette

you consume me
more viciously than fire
obliterates trees

perhaps Juliet's dagger was a metaphor
an illustration of the pain Romeo caused
when she believed he had abandoned her
to the ruins of their poisoned love
to a trickling toxic fume
exchanged between dead lips

at least that's how it feels
each word you choose an aimed bullet
ricocheting through my chest
praying it will strike the core
of this pulsing muscle tissue

you   always liked the taste of blood
sweet like honeydew drops on fresh grass
perhaps that's the only form of love
you ever had for me
a twisted sense of accomplishment
with each mascara-stained droplet
dropping upon previously white sheets

so let's create art
a collage of the pain you caused
with every avoided glance
with every second chance I regret granting
adorned with acrylic paint strokes of realising
I love you   more
than you love me

but this is not how our story ends
you do not get the final pun   the final punch
the final say in how disintegrated
this relationship has become

for once   it's my turn to be the storm

LETTER

I am sorry

perhaps it was wrong of me to fall for you
to pick up the phone and call when I thought of you
to believe there could ever be more to us than an
unseen kiss
or two

you are my secret *maybe*
my lullaby when nights are long
my *once upon a time*

but time has a funny way of escaping us
jumping in its getaway car, pressing the pedal
and rushing astray within a stardust cloud

we knew we could never be
yet I awake to drunken text messages
of *it should've been you & me*
crushing against the walls of reality
begging to be heard

so here I sit
with my choking throat and write
ignoring my spinning thoughts
the knots within my chest
drowning them with shots
of vodka lime

for you were never mine
and I never yours
though we both wish now and then
we could travel back in time
because I know you would've been *perfect*
for the person I used to be
but that's not me anymore

we were a bonfire
which never produced its first sparks
a crackling flame never living long enough
to be extinguished

so I'll sing my lullaby one last time
pretend I'm not dreaming about you when I go to sleep
tonight
and hope that like a butterfly
you will drift away
to someone sweeter

POPCORN

I think I lost you
within a box of honeysuckle popcorn
buckled down with vomit soda and flu-capsule sweets
the ones that look like unicorn treats
and I began to feel a little bit sick

misplaced along a candy wrapper floor
a bacteria war
our eyes remained lip-locked to the movie screen
too keen to notice the people-shaped shadows
held up by toothpicks

for we are no longer children in the dark
with drowned sparks caught in throats that grope for air
feeling our hearts beat within this meat
only when there is a car crash
across the illuminated sheet

so we collided
divided into separate entities
to then re-emerge along misguided thoughts
ordered with extra butter, please
and cheddar cheese
adding each other for flavour

because sometimes life gets a little dull
a constant spur of laughing seagulls
so we escape the traits of our everyday
but my everyday   is you

and while I'm okay with boring Saturday night games
you decided to reclaim your previous fame
chugging foamed caramel with monochrome friends
down at the local disco bar

for you wanted to live in an action film
with gunpowder attraction broken into fractions

while the flames consume our eyes
leaving our hope in a comedy resolution
to coat the garbage-threaded floor of our local Odeon

and I want to puke
whenever I see what Hollywood has made you
an unrelenting trope
the dope of a drama soap
making the *real*
just not enough for you

so we go to the cinema one last time
shoe soles binding with split-slushy enzymes
attempting to rewind to when *we* were still a novelty

at the end of the night we say goodbye
with handshake sighs within a broken night
and then I walk

at least I get to keep the rest of the popcorn

BERGEN

this
is my home
every forest branch and broken bone
every frosted breath and pinecone
intertwined
with roots digging deep
through fairy-tale soil
stained with memory

for it remembers my darkest moments
trails of laughter light as hydrogen
everything I could've been

in another life
I might've stayed
might've found a way to be happy
despite the ever-darkening clouds above head
despite the ways this place seems to drain me

instead I let it slip through my fingertips
blow this city a farewell kiss
and leave

a part of me grieves
knowing now how much happier I can be
even without my loving family
without everything which defined me
for over eighteen years

I'm more confident now
watching small dreams reach reality
laughing at every triviality
recreating my own personality

this
is my origin story
the place I once upon a time
called home

now it's a burial site
for memories I'd prefer to leave six feet deep
for people I never again need to meet
for every night I cried myself asleep

this
is a city
more beautiful than heaven
a landscape more fantastical than any poetry
could attempt to encapsulate

and I loved it
until one day
I outgrew it

BRAASTAD VSOP

make sure you pour me a brandy before I die
and together we will ignore the sounds
of clogged throats coughing beyond the door
of nurses mopping silence as it drizzles down
when little is left to say
leaving us to talk news and TV shows
work and family joys
attempting to smile

pour me a strong coffee with milk and two sugars
while we neglect the presence of a hospital bed
of nurses passing by outside
perhaps the weather is nice
with half-sunshine slicing
through bleached curtain blinds

pour me a strong brandy before I die
and together we can pretend this is a celebratory visit
that you have not discussed my death with doctors
that there is still more time to be merry

and when the clock strikes
I will tell you to go home
to move on with your lives
but before you leave

pour me another strong drink for the night

HOSPITAL

They dress the walls in white. Light too bright for sleep-deprived eyes, and then it's dark – my hollow words swollen in my throat, growing until they become a cyst. Some official-looking person speaks with official-sounding words. The cyst isn't in my throat, but I can feel it.

They assure us they are doing the best they can, yet my mind is unable to understand the mummified manifestation before my eyes. I am looking at a ghost. The transparent fluorescent presence of someone I used to recognise. None of us speak of the dark shadow growing in the corner of the room.

We escape for air at even intervals like a swimmer beneath water. I stare at the coffee machine while dropping cubes of sugar in my tea, a habit to please my restless fingers after having run out of nail polish to scrape off. I hope the nurses don't mind the flakes of red across the floor.

Opening the door becomes a dreaded motion for us. A commotion drained of emotion, unsure how much longer we can continue to feel for. My parents attempt a brave face before they break down and escape, leaving me and my brother alone to converse with the spectre.

We sit in a half-circle around a haunted bed and stare at a sleeping face. I yearn to embrace my teddy bear like I did when I was three, but she isn't here. I look at the others, each fracturing in different patterns like frozen puddles stepped on by school children.

The official-looking people return with more official-sounding words. They ask to speak to the ghost privately. We wait outside. I fill a cup of sugar with warm water and look at withering bouquets forgotten in the haze of passing white shoes making kissing sounds as they step upon the plastic floor.

My father tells me to be prepared. I can see the shadow growing but I pretend it isn't there. I'm not sure there even is such a thing as prepared. And then one day the phone calls.

BROKEN PEOPLE

I see it now

you were damaged in ways
which could never be displayed
along the smooth features of your porcelain face
but I guess in some ways
so was I

for I fell in love
with the glint of broken glass in your eyes
emphasised by the sharp edges of your cracked smile
telling me to calm down whenever I freaked out
while your hands colonised my body

or perhaps *love* is the wrong word

for I could never trust your touch
second-guessing your intentions
revolving in a snowstorm without intervention
wondering if I could ever be more to you
than just a body
more to you
than something to keep you warm at night
more to you
than something you could gaze lustfully at
more to you
than just a thing

but your lips contained magnets
pulling me closer as you became
my preferred prescription of self-harm
your gaze sharper than a blade

though you were not alone in this game
for when we met we smeared mud on our face
creating our own arms race
losing grace at the price
of being better

you were part of my damage
a perpetuator of cracks
despite my hope that you could be salvaged

but broken people are not easy to fix

for broken people have broken dreams
broken brothers and broken genes
drowning in broken bottles in hope
to cope with the broken in me

but you were further along
the trail of destruction than my eyes could see
producing pocket knives for me to slice
my belief in something better

with broken smiles you held me back
threatening neck snap   fact-slap
telling me it was time to press the button
the red one with the warning signs
designed to confine people within their misery
embracing the treachery of dirt
and in the end

I ran

I guess you never wanted to be saved

ALMOST

I never thought
it would come to this

final kisses and goodbye wishes   pressed
between salt-stained lips as we decide
it is better this way

better, we say
despite the pain eroding away
our hearts like nitric acid

despite the seismic shifts
within our ventricles   muscles locked
the slow breaking apart   wondering
if this rift can ever be repaired again

at moments
I want to be mad
to burrow my fists within your chest
my silent confession of distress
even though I could never hurt you

at moments
I regret allowing your words
to cling to air like flies caught
in adhesive tape

at moments
I wish that I was reason enough
for you to plaster together your scattered mind
and figure out what you wanted from life

at moments
I almost regret   loving you

just almost

no longer knowing what to do
with myself

the world appears so far away
behind this network of tears melting
into a kaleidoscope of light

for how can I feel frightened
when the person causing the hurt
feels so much like home?

I almost want to comfort you
despite the pain you place in me
despite the slivers of your voice
still stuck in my arteries

how can I let go?
of a hundred smiling photos
imprinted in my mind
of times when I genuinely believed

this
this is it

you were my first love
you still are
you were my *everything*
but I don't want to be your *almost*

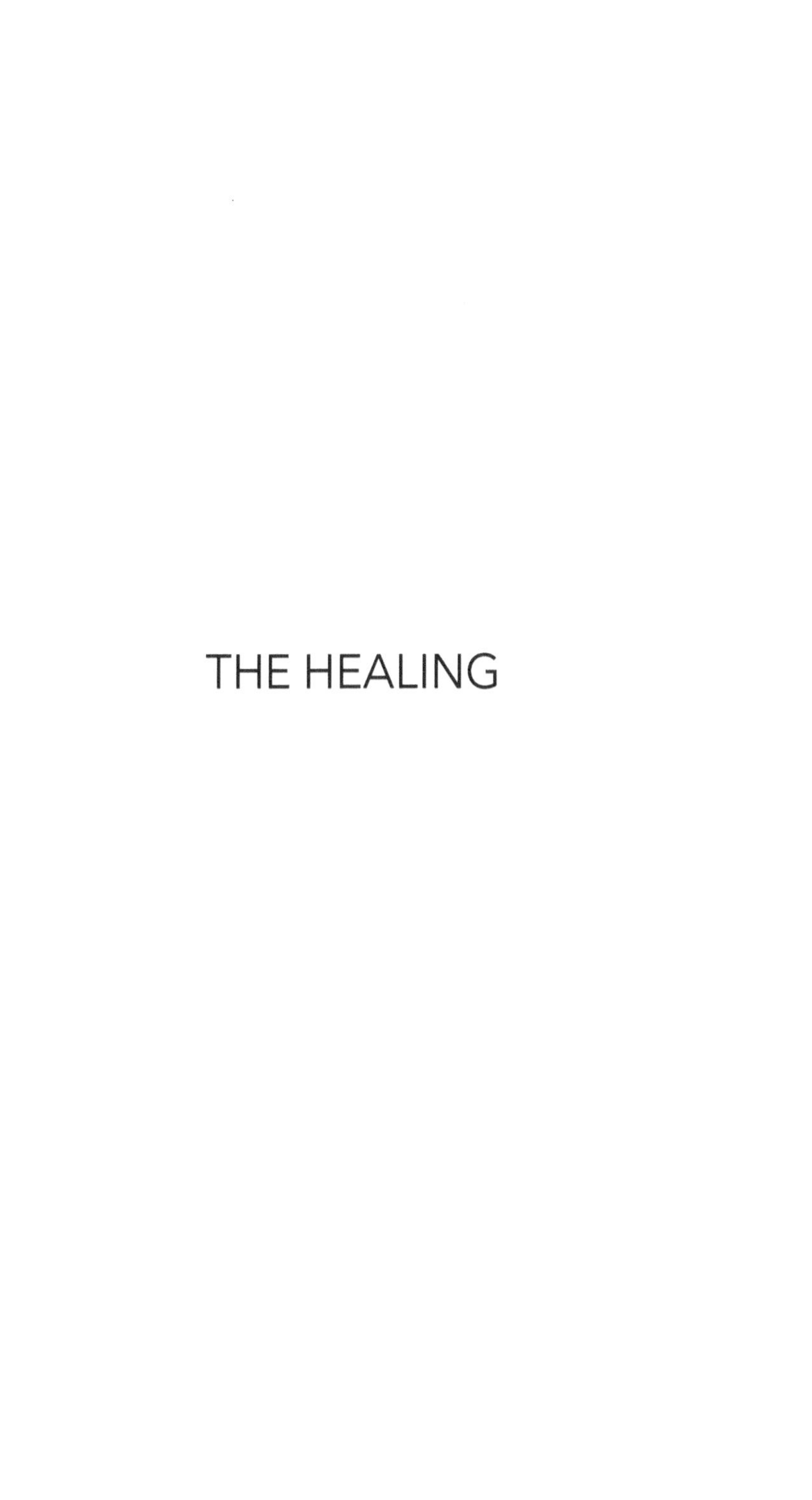

THE HEALING

LØVSTAKKEN[1]

float

       between
       skinned trees

            their peppered dirt
                swamped
           with

      blooming pine-cones

listen while rocks   scribble tales
of trolls

        large as ants, their ember
        spirit subtle against

catalytic birds   swimming

   between

        green

my shoes grow reindeer moss
    food for winter

---

1   Løvstakken is a mountain in Bergen

while an
outdated sun

cries

behind
teddy-bear

neglected
cotton

let fingers caress

bark
its rough cracks

filled with
seams

sparks igniting

tied to childhood roots

KRÅKEBOLLE[2]

With feet crunching neat
against gravel ground, I looked
to clouds, accumulating en
masse, enacting their make-
believe as soldiers preparing
for war, when a droplet landed
on my face.

Wandering through ethereal
grass, I revelled at the clovers,
the telltale hearts of purple
blood as it taints green.

I pointed at a sign, asking him
if it was new.

With tiptoe steps, I reached
the water line. A gentle aquatic
crust floated against undefined
land, its plastic surface slicing a
divide between above

and below. I gave my salute
to a vast kingdom of chalk-
white volcanoes coating rocks
beneath my dry reach.

My brother continued to
the other side, followed by
shadowed remnants of a
forgotten past retracing his
steps.

Standing at the edge we
observed waves giving their
scheduled hugs to rocks below.

---

2   *Kråkebolle* is Norwegian for a type of sea-urchin

Lost in a calm of weathered sky,
I sat down.

I began to feel a hollow tinge: a
dark, guttural lump pestering,
clawing for air. His nails prickled
in my chest, a reminder of his
need for things to end.

I tried not to think, to say
goodbye. While his cries grew
in volume I noticed my brother
shifting at my side.

So I got up.

We found a pond, rain which
never reached the ocean.
Contaminated with waste and
tang, it still encapsulated life.
He pointed out a crab, frozen
still in rusted sea.

And while I glared down at the
small black dots I knew were
his eyes, I thought back to days
when my brother would present
his newfound discoveries
accompanied by a boyish grin
worthy of a hundred lightbulbs.

We ran back to the beach
looking for shells, my fingers
combing through pebble grains
in search of the memories I
once hid in them. Tucked away
at the side, an odd shape,

its colours dreamlike against cream-sun sand.

I picked up a purple sphere dotted with white spikes.

I held it out for him to see, and he began blowing off dust and sand, scraping remnants from its inside.

We wandered back, our eyes greeting a vacant sky. Though gravity tugged and tore, the clouds moved on, mimicking sea as they pulled their battle urges to stranger lands.

Our father told us it was a *kråkebolle*, a common little thing, channelling a buried childlike pride when we presented our newfound treasure.

I placed it where it could have a view of ocean, tucked away in a quiet home, to stay

at least for the moments while we were still here.

MEMORY CHEST

you always allowed me to capture your queen
with serene self-esteem as we played
a round of late-night chess
you with a terry in hand

I knew you couldn't see well at night
distinguish black from white
tower from knight
yet we'd prepare our wooden figures for a fight
and you would let me win

I remember my grandmother complaining
of how you refused to use the new shoes she'd bought
preferring your old wooden clogs
the ones with the giant hole by your big toe
you said it gave some wiggle space

young me thought hiding them would be a great game
forcing you to utilise your unused shoes
confused when told to bring them back
only to repeat the process

ten years ago I forgot their final hideaway
searching your playground basement up and down
I never found them before you passed away

I still haven't

once I found a golden handbag in my grandmother's closet
you teased and said it was yours
that you needed it when you waltzed into town
in a dress and gown
ready to sing karaoke

we laughed for half an hour

I miss your cooking

always served with a tad too much pepper
as all six of us would gather around a table
five feels too lonely a number now

I remember a time when I was playing the piano
you listening from the kitchen and asking
with towel in hand about a song you didn't recognise

I'll never forget the smile that grew
from within your eyes
like a beaming light unable to hide its shine
when I told you it was mine
I'd made it up

I've now inherited your accordion
you'd laugh watching my fingers fumble
frantically across its button keyboard
making sounds but not sense

I wonder what you'd think of the changes we've made
an attic free from termites and a garden filled with rocks
not to mention the vegetarian robot feeding off your lawn
my grandmother calls it *the toad*

a part of me thinks you feel calm
knowing we are taking care of her

we were both fond of gardening
the peace as a bee breezes by
hands in dirt and watching plants decide
where and whether they'll grow into place

your workshop exudes magic
walls covered with tools I could never name
just waiting for the initial spark
to begin the arc of creation
mumbling in a language I cannot comprehend

you've left me with so many memories
I like to believe I carry a piece of you in my heart
safe and stored away for a cloudy day
you always knew how to make me smile

from ash to ash
with love

PS:
my cheeks are still permanently scarred
from the time when at a restaurant
you tried to explain to me
what foot flirting was

THINGS YOU SHOULD KNOW BEFORE WE MOVE IN TOGETHER

1.
there will be hair everywhere
imagine small, brown-furred Furbies
clotting the shower drain as a mountain
of shampoo builds up surrounded by a lake

2.
if you hear me scream as if I'm being murdered
it just means I've spotted a spider roaming our apartment
rent-free. if possible I will force you to evict said squatter
while standing upon a chair performing my ceremonial
cringe dance

3.
you will know I've been occupying a room
when it is left dishevelled with stacks of books
a teacup with circular orange stains, a pool of papers
nail polish, speaker, scissors, glue, pen, headphones
computer, hairband, camera, leaves
pressed flowers and a comfy sweater

4.
my holy grail/bible
is my complete works of William Shakespeare
(not the Norton one, the other one)
do not touch

5.
there will be no need to buy coffee tables
with my 167 books and your 149
we will reinvent the idea of book storage
by stacking them up to create surfaces
upon which to place our tea
though if we spill…

6.
let me make it perfectly clear
that my mind does not recognise such trivialities
as a *my* and *your* side of the bed
you will lie down on one spot
and I will cling on to you like anemones on rocks
I would claim the drifting sea of sheets scares me
but we both know you are the human equivalent of a radiator

7.
one day you will start snoring
considering you fall asleep in three seconds
while I need half an hour, I'll do my best
not to suffocate you with a pillow
because that's what love is

8.
expect me to ramble
and lose sight of what
I was trying to say

9.
expect me to go crazy decorating whenever Halloween,
Christmas, Easter, the Norwegian national day, New Year's
Eve, someone's birthday, promotion, parents visiting, spring,
autumn, cat jumps upon the couch, Bonfire Night, change in
clocks, I found my bracelet underneath the toaster, dinner is
ready, remember to buy milk, OMG I saw the cutest video on
Facebook where –
what was I talking about again?

10.
I will continue my duty as a girlfriend
and jump on you like a ninja when you least expect it
providing you with a multitude of heart attacks

11.
we will probably have to dedicate a room
to all the random things I bring back with me from nature:
seashells, sand, pebbles, leaves, flowers, branches, bugs
the neighbours' cat, that cute fox I saw that one night
trees, ants, bunnies, bears...

12.
knowing me and knowing you
our kitchen will be a collage of squeaky clean
and a Pisa tower composed of unwashed dishes
now, let's not make any assumptions
regarding who cleaned what and made what mess
but don't you agree the pizza plate, spaghetti bowl
crumb-riddled platter, teacup, noodle pot, wine glass
and frying pan piazza is kinda impressive?

13.
finally – if you are able to put up with my list
I may find it in my heart to tolerate yours

14.
finally, finally – I love you

SONNET CXV

I cannot grant you my kingfish kisses while flamingos with tyrant umbrellas plaster propaganda on wet walls, protesting deductions sung by sacred bees in interludes, lips lost in a centrifuge of important talk concerning thingamabobs and thoraxes, eyes betraying evidence of characteristic deficiencies in kittens, your vowels keep me in 'twixt when my mind shifts among altering thistles, lost between your changeling dedications of kingdom, attempting to reclaim our escaped timekeeper with a million accolades before we're trapped within its xylophone.

ODE TO THE FEMALE ARTIST

this is a *thank you*
to the blood you drew across each canvas
battling with a pen dipped in ink
continuing despite being pushed beyond
the brink of giving up

thank you for never surrendering
to pleas for you to quit but rather rendering
them your satiric subject
screaming out a call to arms
against a drought of female artistry

thank you to Deborah Harkness
for showing me a heroine, an academic
a witch, a time-traveller, a mother, a warrior
against segregation and a champion of love

thank you to Kate Mosse
for revealing the power of history
remembrance and adventure

thank you to Vanessa Diffenbaugh
for blooming my passion for flowers
for being truthful about the difficulties of trust
the unpleasant realities of birth
and the coldness of dirt at night

thank you to Amalie Skram
the champion of my home town
for conveying your experience of being trapped
within a mental asylum against your will

thank you to Mary Shelley
for inspiring the Promethean flame
still burning in my heart

thank you to Kate Chopin
for showing me a woman independent

from her failed marriage
a lover of art and mystery
following her passions even to the end
of the ocean

thank you to the female authors and poets
inspiring me every day with their creations
for continuing to write even at your lowest
for raising your voice and daring to be unladylike
striking down the boundaries telling us
what we can and cannot do

for reminding me
we can do *everything*

thank you

TRUTH

they say there is truth in poetry
I say there is truth in every atom
every molecule attached to your kiss
small grains of the universe trapped
between your lips and mine

you can find truth unfurling through concrete
as a new daffodil learns to yearn for the sun
watching it stretch forth knowing nothing
but its desire for warmth

you can find truth in music
pirouetting along bittersweet tunes of dusty pianos
their tangents tangoing the way rain tap-dances on grass
a melody which has been playing for centuries

truth is the comfort of your warm body
whispering midnight pleas for me to never leave
so I sleep sweetly with you to protect me against bad dreams
before I wake up alone

truth is believing in something greater than us all
something so divine it exists only to retain the rules of life
a reason to believe that everything will be alright
as it observes us wandering blind

truth is watching bouquets unfold in the streets
memories and tokens placed in grace
ready to embrace the heartbroken
marking the place where life used to sing its melodies

truth is where there is truth no more
fought for in war zones because truth has become a delicacy
so rare it's now rationed only for dirt and stone
displaced between bomb sirens in drop zones

truth is me whispering *I love you*

through the crackling on the phone
and truth is wishing you'd said more
than *I'm sorry*

truth is the friends who pick you up when you are down
who hold you tight when things aren't right
who make you remember everything
still worth fighting for

truth is relearning to love the human race
to watch the embrace of strangers
their kindness spreading like wildfire
through our concrete heaven

truth is knowing
I'll never be more than my words
that my birth came with an expiration date
but still finding the courage to live

I'd say truth is watching sparks of dust
dance through the first moments of sunrise
knowing that no matter what came before
today is a new day

I LOVE YOU

at first the words sound like sugar plums
far too sweet as they tickle across your tongue
inching their way out

I never feared saying them to you
rather revered the thought of saying them too soon
so I kept them locked up for as long as I could
before they found a key and slipped out
through my teeth

I love you

I can still feel my tummy
bubbling like champagne
as you look me in the eyes
and say the same

with time the words grew to sound like home
whispered along late night streets
and between bedroom sheets
as we fell asleep comfortably
next to each other's heartbeat

your words were decorated
with amalgamated speculations
exploring the feather-light possibilities
of us having a life together

until one day they were gone
replaced by a metallic aftertaste
as I swallowed bullets instead

I can still hear them clinking in my stomach
the churning of insecurity after my home was ripped away
instead replaced by the frosty winter wind

now they're blood plums
as I trace the cuts across my tongue
where the words once used to dance
debating the chance of the wounds ever healing enough
for me to place trust in them again

A1

The road was static – cinematic as we passed layers of green and yellow coating the road's shoulders, guiding us further into autumn. Together we counted miles as they passed beneath our feet and uttered long tales to fill our ears as a string of red lights gathered up before us.

A *friend of a friend who lived in the woods / with dwindling weeds annexing roundabouts / we get more human when the road slows down / sliced off a bit of his thigh and fried it / this is where I'd climb on top of the roof and dance / apparently it tasted like pork / there's an ebook called* Trump and the Bellboy *where / lets send all the vapes to Mars! / his oily orange skin glistening in the sunlight as if he were a soggy Cheeto / have you ever just dropped dead in the middle of / everything in this country is trying to fuck you / dressed up as a huge donkey dick for elections evening / we love efficient bitches! / sounds of saturation crackling through the radio / two fields of white and red flowers / I once drove with my legs crossed / for we are no longer visiting an idea, but a person / true patience is not believing in time / for horoscopes are truthful lies / 'Eat your vegetables!' she yelled. 'Languorously' / he spoke beneath the shadow of windmills / I love that their 'fucks' rhymes with 'socks' / we play twenty questions with signs of highway maintenance / I spy with my little eye something that starts with / our car catches up with a tank of liquid nitrogen / service in half a mile / what is fluffy like mashed potato, but immaterial / if you can't see my mirrors I can't see you / no contours but bright lights / if you drink me you die / if I leave you here / tiredness can break / anything to stop this turning on and off again / spilling my drink over my city / we recycle used cooking oil / you're such an ear! / a souring / sound like a dog being dragged backwards through an electric fence / imagine: Willy Wonka and the Slaughterhouse Factory.*

With 210,000 miles logged within the car's meter it was 30,000 short of having travelled to the surface of the moon.

THE PEOPLE'S BOOKSHOP

through the narrow streets and up the steep stairs
we find Durham's socialist bookshop
huddled within an attic our eyes gaze sideways
along bookshelf-covered walls and out
the thin windows and into the plaza below

caught between an old red-bound copy
of Aristotle's masterpieces and a pillow-soft book
containing the poetical works of Elizabeth Barrett Browning
I surrender myself to a world of literature
lost within a tempest of words

we dress up in top hats and long coats
while parading around the shop in quest of ideas
embodying Emerson's transparent eye
as we survey the content of our palms

between the covers of *Alice Leighton*
a book adorned by baby blue and velvet printed berries
I find an inscription to Margaret J Watson dated July 30th
1896
I wonder how long she kept that novel
before passing it along

enwrapped by a spotted copy of Dostoyevsky's *The Devils*
I fade away into a world of time-tanned pages
smelling of nothing but home and revel
when two hundred pages in the wise serpent emerges
crawling out to offer a bouquet of pressed grass

my friends all buzz around me
one lost to extremist propaganda
claiming men to be reproductively redundant
while another flicks through protest photos and stops
at an image of a man taking a selfie
with an explosion in the background

our hostess Gabs offers tea and coffee
before switching on the heat
filling the air with the familiar scent of burnt dust
while we giggle at postcard and coaster riddles

as the kettle brews we dance
through years of politics placed into words
and pirouette despite the shop's small enclosure
before settling down to warm our hands on hot mugs

not before long
Durham's already cold air chills down
so we pick up our departure and say our goodbyes
to the socialist bookshop
hidden within cobbled streets

17TH MAY

I strapped the belt tight
around my waist, faced
with being displaced on the day
on which my country portrays its grace
with festive means
to celebrate the day
we erased our ties
to other allies, to create
something of our own

I dragged my friends with me
to Southwark Park, to hear the tongue
in which I'd been deprived, to revive
my sense of pride in country
they bought me a flag to wave
when I couldn't bring my own
too big to fit in any suitcase

I came up the Underground stairs
a Norwegian princess
holding my woollen skirt high
so not to trip while I skip
towards something familiar

for nothing rang better
than when a stranger smiled and said
gratulerer med dagen[3] in the middle
of a busy street, a sweet treat
to homesick ears

we found grass
filled with Nordic tunes
stuffing faces with food

---

3   *Gratulerer med dagen* is Norwegian for
        congratulations, used both for birthdays and as a
        greeting on our national day

I'd forgotten I knew

I left in order to experience another life
stomaching fear of losing touch with my tongue
and the sounds it used to make
for when I miss my language
I miss my family, my friends
the store employee who says *hello*
in a different way

but today
I get to experience it all again

WATERLOO EAST

With feet on mosaic streets I dissolve into a vapour of individuals gushing past from side to side, like water molecules bouncing through air, jumping on and off bus rides coughing up enough carbon dioxide to choke a forest.

Floating down Cornwall Road I encounter a transparent stag. I watch as it munches grime from flowerbeds long ago converted into ashtrays by chain-smokers out at night having a puff, illuminated by the glow of the pub where their mates remain inside chugging chrome-yellow house ale.

The mailman trots from home to home, delivering parcels to doors coloured in fractured light as he walks along the rainbow in a street with letters and late-night drunken Amazon purchases from anywhere between here and Baltimore.

I trace the lines of my palm towards Blackfriars, lost in a world no longer mine as I become a foreigner in a new city, walking through a network of dialects as a tennis court sign reminds me to exhale construction noise.

I tread over displaced cardboard and greet hotel employees smoking their lunchtime cigarettes below a *Danger of Death* sign while my lungs fill with the distinct smell of sour tarmac being laid down to pave new pathways for the blindly rushing businessmen from Suffolk preaching randomly generated numbers into their phones.

No longer hidden by a forest of buildings, I watch as a naval fleet of red double-deckers drift by, alerting me of each new theatre and film production available soon, now, or somehow last week, before finding myself transformed into a lone electron in a sea of charged personalities within a copper wire designed to transmit electricity.

We amalgamate along Union Street to the buzz of hummingbirds disappearing off to work.

Losing fraction after fraction of myself I follow behind natives brazenly jaywalking, merging with their shadows as I retrace the steps of a phosphorous Frank O'Hara as his ghost continues its tour around Europe. The two of us disappear within an empty square, breathing fresh air void of humans before the next wave washes in again and we continue on our separate ways.

I play I-spy with St Paul's through skyscrapers, tiptoeing around builders as they shift the skyline left and right. Looking up I yearn to know what's inside these massive hives of lives, the secrets they keep inside and whether or not they binge-watch *Friends* as much as I do. A door opens to my right and my heart twinges as a lone office clerk abandons a box of pink lilies in a skip next to the Globe.

Once the sun has vaporised I repeat my steps back to Waterloo East. I become a moving reflection across coffee house windows as I fade away among waves of black umbrellas along the South Bank. The buildings capture the sky's remaining light like fireflies in mason jars placed on display along their windows.

The construction workers have now gone home. St Paul remains unmoved. The hotel employees have stubbed out their cigarettes. And the cardboard along the pavement is now wet.

WILL YOU WRITE ABOUT ME?

found poetry based on Han Suyin's A Many-Splendoured Thing

will you love   grass

in abundant sun   stretched

      to granite

          below wrinkled sea

alone

          in endless spring

             we spoke

of the splitting   from

                    voices calm

too full of anything   but

            you   within   me

or some other good reason

              I'd sell love

         for reason

       does not seem

     sacrilege to sell   hot passion

his fingers along odours

of memories

I shall write

how we loved

I'll exhume the sea's

tide littered with   hurt

done to me

as I scratch torpid   scars

of ecstasy

KINTSUGI

they ask us how we made it
they ask us how through thick and thin
scraping at the outermost rims of life
we fought to keep it

I tell them we used gold

I tell them
just because we break
doesn't mean it's time to forsake
everything we have

what's broken can be golden

those fractures can embolden us
at times when just holding on is tough enough
without the hurt of us breaking up

our cracks can make us stronger
fight even longer for what we know is right
encourage the other to conquer the world
through whispered words at night

through thick and thin
you hold my hand understanding
neither of us can discover Wonderland
on our own

our flaws are our perfection

a collection of the moments
which brought us closer
a display of affection resurrected
whenever we are close enough to giving up

I know you are no Prince Charming
but you rinse my wounds when I am hurt
and assert that you still love me

you will tell me
to follow those wild dreams of mine
even if it means leaving you behind
but I won't

because together we are better
together we can face
whatever weather chance
can cast our way

let our display of love
showcase that whenever one stumbles astray
the other can illuminate their pathway home

so let our fingers trace the golden veins
despite the wounds this porcelain love
still remains

for as long as one can hold the pieces
and the other the golden glue
there will always be
a me & you

ACKNOWLEDGEMENTS

It's no secret I've referred to the past few years of my life as simultaneously the best and the worst. While you've now been privy to a lot of my scribbled heartache, I'd like to take this opportunity to thank everyone who's been part of sparking a myriad of laughter.

Thank you to several generations of the University of Kent Creative Writing Society. You became my family away from home, my encouragers when I'd yet to learn to raise my voice, my supporters as I transformed within the role as president, my co-conspirators as we stumbled across foreign cobbled streets and my film-buddies as we huddled up in the English room for yet another midnight movie. There is not a single day where I don't miss every one of you. ¨

Thank you to the Canterbury poetry community for taking me under your wings as I stumbled through words on stage and for blessing me with countless opportunities to develop. This book wouldn't have been possible without all of you.

Thank you to the friends who spent evening after evening listening as I talked through whatever was currently going on in my life, who always had a shoulder ready for me to cry on and whom never seize to astonish me with their cheery silliness and warming smiles.

Thank you to the university lecturers who opened my eyes to the possibilities of poetry and whom saw something in me I couldn't see myself.

Thank you to my family – I know this is not what you had envisioned for me, but unfortunately the position as engineer/lawyer/botanist was taken, so poet it is.

www.ingramcontent.com/pod-product-compliance
Lightning Source LLC
Chambersburg PA
CBHW021345060726
47591CB00006B/2163